Earth Soldier

by Don Robinson

Earth Soldier
Relationships Define Our Purpose

earthsoldierlifestyle.com
By Don Robinson Copyright © 2017

ISBN: 978-0-9826994-3-0

All rights reserved. No parts of this book may be reproduced in any form without permission in writing from the publisher, except by a reviewer who may quote brief passages for reviewing purposes.

Acknowledgments

I would like to thank family and friends for their love and support. I want to acknowledge my three grandmothers, Ophelia, Alma, and Annie Bell, for showing me where wisdom hides. Man can lock down our bodies but our minds are free to grow forever Lavert. If you ever find yourself surrounded by doubt, and I'm not physically in your presence, remember I'll be praying for you. I will be meditating on your behalf and asking the Creator to deliver the vision, knowledge, courage, and love you need to keep pressing forward. It should be clear to you by now Nazeer, that even though we may not always agree, our bond is enduring like the bond between the Earth and Moon.

This book is inspired by many things. My family, community, and travels serve as catalyst for inspiration. My grandmothers left their parents, siblings, and life on the farm for the hope of better economic opportunites in the city of Richmond, VA. I am grateful for the decades spent with all three of my grandmothers.

They struggled to gain equal employment rights, made sacrifices to serve their community, and raised a family.

They were forced to innovate and maximize the limited resources at their disposal. These women fought through relentless gender discrimination and economic exploitation. Their faith and ingenuity helped them care for their families in a hostile American social system. At the core of our struggles are a wealth of lessons we receive through the bonds that define relationships. These bonds link us to people, ambitions and ultimately to our life's purpose.

Table of Contents

Introduction 1
The Power of Relationships 3
Approaching Each Day 4
The Power of Metaphors 7
In Search of Comfort 9
Nature as a Model 11
Destined 16
Letters Written to The Spirit..17
IT 24
This Mind of Mine 25
The Powerful Union (English Version).....................................26
Millennium Queen of Heaven 27
Excerpt from the poem: 189 Travels with Xes...........................28
Excerpt from the poem: Love Fantasy.......................................29
Pink Sunshine Emotions..30
My Angel the Ageless Jewel...31
Excerpt from the poem: What is the profit of a mind that gains the world and forgets about the soul?...........................32
Excerpt from the poem: The Millennium Season of Autumn 33
N.F.B.T.I..34
Earth Soldier 35
777 sages ago 36
Look hard enough and..37
Insert from the poem: Afronectar Verse 7: 9-13.......................38
My queen needs to know...39
My king needs to know 41

I am the last of the worshippers
I am the last of my kind
I am the last of the followers
I have found my peace of mind

Esthero
"Indigo Boy"

Introduction

The reflections, meditations, and poetry in this book fuse together the beauty and divinity of our natural environment. Humanity shares a common destiny through an obvious bond with Earth. The Planet Earth is occasionally referred to as Gaia throughout this book. Gaia, the great mother, nurtures and assists in sustaining humanity's relationship with the Creator. *Earth Soldier* offers a perspective while raising questions about the relationship we have with our communities and the planet. The content found in this book revisits the understanding of how cycles impact our lives. Personal and collective experiences define impressionable moments that life burns into our psyche as important reminders. Reflecting on those moments remind us that situations and emotions are all subject to change. The same unpredictability expressed in our planet's weather patterns is a mirror reflection of the unexpected changes that occur in relationships with people and communities.

What is true today may not be relevant tomorrow. To what degree is life's uncertainty responsible for fueling a desire for comfort or meaning? The perspective that frames an answer to this question defines our attitude toward life. The bad luck that sticks hard on Monday can surely get replaced with a powerful jolt of positive energy by Friday.

In a time of escalating global conflicts, confrontational words and deeds take center stage in our conversations. Even though many of the poems and affirmations in this book were written in the decade of The 1990s, their meaning is constantly evolving. There are occasions when revisiting perspectives from the past, assists with forming solutions to the problems that exist today. It is common knowledge that spending too much time in the past is counterproductive. However, the lessons we have collected along the way illuminate with insight and provide a path from a place of confusion to a place of personal discovery. Furthermore, poetry conveys abstract ideas more clearly and serves as a way to transfer the depth of the emotions behind written words. Inevitably, our ability to suc-cessfully communicate a point of view, favors the opinion of the person receiving the message.

If the message being communicated isn't tailored for the person hearing the message, it will likely fall upon deaf ears. Every person reading this book has a common destiny with the heartbeat of Earth. The format of this book takes that understanding into consideration. The intent going forward is that the visual learners will see meaningful images and metaphors embedded in the poetry. The auditory learners will hear the rhythm of the messages being conveyed. Finally, those who learn with emotional intelligence will feel the passion and commitment expressed throughout this book.

The Power of Relationships

Relationships whisper meaning into our lives. These relationships must assist in cultivating those inner gifts given to us by the Creator. We are sent to Earth for a reason. That reason is buried and defined in experiences we share with people and the environment. What makes a relationship transform into a "powerful union" is the awareness people share regarding their duty to one another. This transformation starts with discovering the duty, role, and level of self-awareness required in order to maintain important relationships. The more we learn about ourselves, the more empowered we become and capable of understanding our responsibilities. Reflect on the level of conviction society has for passing on a safe, inhabitable planet to our children for a moment. The ability to refine one's thinking is initiated by reflecting on the values that fuel wants and desires. The transition from self-awareness to self- empowerment moves us toward identifying and fulfilling important obligations that are associated with relationships. This transition provides the necessary insight for understanding the nature of those intimate bonds that sustain relationships. Potentially this discovery process will assist with reaching a level of mental and emotional clarity.

Approaching Each Day

Everyday we rise (ASCENSION) and try to maintain some type of consistency in our lives (SUSPENSION). Sometimes we experience the feeling of losing control that causes fear and doubt to arise (THE DESCENT). Inevitably we (FALL) in order that our faith is tested. If we are willing to see it, lingering somewhere in our lowest moment dwells the (DELIVERANCE). Let us seek to elevate the human compassion that arises from our daily struggles so one day we may all rise again.

The impressions we leave on people are lasting. It's impossible to please everyone, so try not to worry over situations that you have no control over. However, we do have control over how we treat people. By raising our level of self-awareness, we are empowered to calm the appetite for destruction. This destructive appetite is usually fueled by personal insecurites. In turn, this newly reached level of self-awareness will elevate our emotional state. It's easy to fear the unknown and difficult to tame insecurities. When like minds are in tune with higher order needs and desires, the gates of heaven will open and invite conscious souls into experiencing the pleasure of the ages.

When this experience is revealed, embrace it and delight in the moment. Remember, this experience isn't promised to us all. This moment of bliss is only promised to self-aware individuals who seek to transform their perspectives and values. The level of self-awareness being described in this book is holistic. Relationships with other people are no more important than our relationship with the environment. This is an interesting perspective because few of us ever consider our relationship with Gaia. Our ego directs us to focus on relationships that offer immediate gratification. If we define our vulnerabilities according to the dependence we have on the planet, the influence of the ego will decline. Ordinarily, it's the ego that gives personal insecurities power. When our relationship with Gaia is properly acknowledged, the human ego has less influence on the bonds that sustain our relationships with one another and the planet. The least among us are just as important as the greatest because we all are susceptible to the same fate. It becomes obvious that we are at the mercy of Gaia's divine rotation. Since we are at the mercy of these laws, let us raise our awareness by studying those natural laws that govern our destiny.

The Journey

…could life be a journey guided into a quest, made to be truth, tortured by reality, censored by perception, perfected by the thinker?

The Power of Metaphors

Metaphors are powerful because words can transform the way we understand and relate to the world. Gaia is a metaphor for complex systems and atmospheric relationships that sustain our lives on this planet. The ancestors, humanity's mothers, and fathers clearly viewed the Earth symbolically as a goddess or great mother. When certain longings, emotions or complex relationships are difficult to convey, metaphors can offer a solution. Religious books are filled with metaphors and symbolism that convey important lessons. What can we learn from the metaphors our ancestors used to convey their relationship with Earth? The road that humanity has been traveling is overpopulated with questions that haunt us from the cradle to the grave.

The relationships we develop measure our commitment to obtaining answers for pressing questions. In addition, these relationships shed light on the kinds of comfort we seek. Do we surround ourselves with people who must constantly say things to appease us or people who look to challenge our positions and force us to grow into wiser, more knowledgeable citizens?

In Search of Comfort

Many people travel through life seeking a pleasure principle that exists only in dreams. There are many things that we do and names that we use to identify and find comfort. The communities that we live in are supposed to offer some level of comfort. The Garden of Eden on some level can be considered a metaphor that conveys that message. If we seek to build a partnership with our natural world, then, as a result, we might experience a greater level of comfort. We must work to create a healthy environment that comforts us mentally, physically, and emotionally. This job isn't easy, but it deserves our attention and effort. We can build a consensus to improve our community interactions by creating incentives for planting gardens and removing random garbage from the streets and sidewalks. Our local organizations can partner to form these green initiatives.

Nature as a Model

Today, in many cases, our churches avoid making accommodations for the role nature plays in our understanding of the Divine. The Christian mind typically associates the Divine with the story of Jesus. Seldom does the topic of protecting Gaia on behalf of nature's divinity take center stage. This is understandable, because I assume church sermons focus on the moral obligation associated with reaching heaven after death. However, if we look at the Christian bible from an environmental perspective, then the life of Jesus was sustained by the forces of nature. How often do we hear stories about nature being celebrated as an active participant or partner in man's search for the Divine? Did nature only play a subservient role to the wishes of men during the time of Jesus? Were these men enlightened? Did they ever speak about a special relationship with nature? Did the common knowledge in the Middle East 2000 years ago include the fact that birds were vital to the pollination process and that the food supply is dependent on this natural process? Human beings are not successful at surviving on this planet without nature's assistance. We benefit from relationships with animals, insects, and plants. We were given the power to subdue extensions of the natural world by God. This power was loaned to us based on our promise to assist in managing and sharing the bounty of the planet with all of God's creations.

In biblical times, I assume people were mindful of nature's divinity. Initially, religious understanding and wisdom were derived from an appreciation of the natural world. People and communities constructed an idea of how the spiritual world operated by studying nature. This line of reasoning highlights the role nature plays in advancing critical thinking and spiritual development. Without Gaia, we would cease to exist as a species and have no way to ascertain the inner workings of creation. Using the lessons we receive in church only for reacting to

Satan's attack on moral principles, ignoring Earth's divinity, limits the positive influence churchgoers can have on the world. Our purpose and potential as parents, citizens, and worshipers should align with protecting the environment, God's most precious gift. Protecting Gaia is part of a moral obligation. The sermons extracted from religious texts by our spiritual leaders must encourage followers to study and learn the laws of nature. These laws are modeled to reflect the inner workings of the Divine. Human beings are no more than an extension of nature.

The story of biblical figures isn't just about the deeds of men. The symbolism behind feeding the masses with a fish and a loaf of bread represents the inseparable bond between nature and the Divine. If the water that housed the fish was polluted, do you think Jesus would have made a comment about the polluted water source? Do you know of any religious writings that help us define our relationship with Earth?

Progress can be made in protecting the environment by helping younger generations better understand their practical relationship with nature. For example, Mrs. Obama took a step in this direction by inviting children from D.C. to assist in planting a garden on the White House lawn. The event probably made an impression on the kids who participated and piqued interest in health and wellness. Places of worship can support a realignment of thinking by organizing a nine-week summer camp that teaches children how to plant seeds and maintain a garden. This simple activity can teach generations of children how to live healthier. In addition to gaining a healthier lifestyle, children can learn basic principles of economics by assigning a monetary value to the finished product, which is the labor invested and the vegetables harvested from the garden. In my opinion, churches are strategic assets because they have the philosophical, logistical, structural, and human resources already in place. This idea can only be implemented if local green organizations lend their expertise in leadership roles.

Training children how to operate a vegetable stand introduces customer service and teamwork principles. Teaching them to grow, maintain and assign a financial value to the food production process has an unlimited number of benefits for participants and the community. Above all, the techniques needed for starting and maintaining a garden are symbolic of what is needed for sustaining spiritual growth.

According to Genesis, Gaia was created in the beginning with the Creator's words and imagination. Teaching a child universal lessons and principles of spiritual growth are facilitated by using metaphors associated with garden care and maintenance. The deification or personification of Earth in discussions can help children and adults better understand our relationship with the natural environment. Reading, writing, arithmetic, technology, and knowledge of nature provide a solid foundation and a great learning experience. The children in our communities must embrace and respect their relationship with nature.

Humanity's relationship with nature's divine principle was expressed using symbols drawn on pyramids and cave walls thousands of years ago. The divinity in nature was also expressed in ancient text with metaphors that conveyed universal spiritual meanings. Even our economic systems are built around the assumption that nature will continue fulfilling her bountiful purpose. The right knowledge equips the younger generation with an ability to offer innovate solutions for 21st century problems.

I am an extension of my environment. Caring for the environment is just as important as caring for our personal relationships. Your relationship with loved ones is sustained and at times enhanced by the power of our natural world. Our lives are defined and redefined by the ebb and flow that exists within our relationships. Thanking someone for a gift is a natural impulse. When we lend our attention, we make a conscious decision to become more aware. As our awareness grows, our ability to practice empathy or disregard our responsibilities grows more acute. Growing the knowing part of our existence takes work. Each day we grow more self-aware, conscious of our roles, thoughtful and introspective of the influence we have on the environment. Gaining this basic understanding is important during our journey on Earth. The planet provides the experiences needed to increase self-awareness and encourage growth. The fruit in the Garden of Eden came from a tree that was sustained by Gaia's relationship with her purpose. Just like plants, we all need nurturing and space to grow. The descendants of indigenous populations around the world are imprisoned by pollution. Imperialism has left its mark in many ways; pollution is the most apparent by-product of Imperialism. We can change this reality and offer a cleaner, smarter reality for cities and countrysides within this Knowledge Economy.

The backdrop to our unfolding human drama on this planet is the relationship between the Sun, Moon, and Earth. How will our endeavors be interpreted by occupants of the planet hundreds of years from now? What kind of wisdom will we offer the generations to come? How will our relationship with the planet be interpreted by our sons and daughters? Will our relentless pursuit of artificial intelligence align with the laws of nature? The American educational system struggles to offer adequate solutions for solving 21st century social problems. How can we use scientific research to create a better quality of life if our learning systems lack diversity of thought?

Destined

Make a point to study the bonds that define important relationships. We are destined to learn from the positive and negative experiences in life. The more conscious we are about these experiences, the more we will be able to create and sustain a productive relationship with each other, our communities, and the environment as a whole. Each day, we are for -tunate that Gaia provides for us as we evolve into the awareness of our purpose. It's important that we actively seek out answers to important questions. The corporate media engine in America will offer answers. It's a personal decision to accept or reject those answers offered by media outlets. Remember that the source of these answers should exist within.

Letters Written to The Spirit

The relationships we develop measure our commitment to obtaining answers for pressing questions.

How are you doing? I hope that this letter reach you in the best of health. I am doing okay so far. It is 8am and I'm in a cafe eating break-fast. I miss you so much, which is more than I expected to. It's funny because I've only known you for a month, but it feels a lot longer than that and during that month you've made me do nothing but smile. You've hon-estly touched a special place in my heart. Normally, I wouldn't be telling you any of this because that would mean admitting that I do like you, but I am growing, and I realize that there's no point in holding things back and maybe regret it later.

I know we've both been holding things back from each other (thoughts and feelings) especially our feelings because neither of us want-ed to get hurt and who could blame us knowing that because, I was getting ready to leave. Well, that's a part of life, and they say everything happens for a reason. I don't know what the reason is for us being thrown together in such a short space of time, but I do have to say that it made me realize that not all men are completely bad. They're far from perfect but not all bad. Thank you far that. Maybe that was the reason we were put together. I hope you see it and understand what I am saying.

There were a lot of times we've been together relaxing or whatever and many of those times you've asked me what I was thinking. The truth is, (and brace yourself) I was thinking about you, and the reason I always told you otherwise was because, I would have to let you in. I wasn't prepared to do that.

I tried so hard not to put any kind of feelings or emotions into what we were doing and just go with the flow, but you made that so hard for me. You had to go and be nice didn't you? I was prepared for the worst, and instead I got the best. I had a lot of questions toward the end because I wanted to see what kind of person you really were.

Any ways as I was saying before, I wasn't prepared to let you into my heart because that would mean getting hurt in the end, and I noticed you weren't doing much either to let me into your heart, mainly for the same reasons. I think we're all scared of getting hurt but life is also full of regrets, and I don't want this to be one of them. I am now in Puerto Rico, and I have an hour to kill before they start boarding my flight. So any ways are you pretty shocked by my letter up to this point or is this what you were more or less expecting? It doesn't matter because I've got more to say. To tell you the truth no one's ever made me feel the way you did. In the short space of time that I've known you, you've made me feel like someone so special. You've made me feel beautiful, appreciated, because of you. I know that I can do and deserve much better than what I've been getting. No one appreciated me the way that you did. In fact, past relationships have made me doubt myself, doubt my confidence, my self-worth, my looks, everything. You made me realize even more what I've always known and that was that, I am a beautiful person both in and out, and I only deserve the best. Thank you.

You don't realize how much you have done for me, and it wasn't just the compliments, it was the way you made me feel both inside and out. If nothing else, I do hope we can remain friends forever, and I hope nothing but the best for you in life.

---many relationships leaving you divided and unfocused---

First your relationships are a source of knowledge, and you love to learn. Therefore, the more relationships you have the more you learn. This can be real pressure for those who come into contact with you to remain a source of information, but it can also be stimulating for them to stay in-formed.

The question becomes will you ever be satisfied with one person -one sole source of information? According to my great aunt's astrology book, a Gemini's true desire and goal in life is to find his soul mate. All I ask is what does a soul mate look like, feel like, act like -how will you know? Apparently, all the relationships are only the outcome of you searching for a soul mate.

-Restlessness

Asia and I were discussing this the other day because we both become bored so quickly! Celestine Prophecy also touches on this in the "Critical Mass chapter." Restlessness is caused by knowing there is something more, yet not knowing what it is! The more knowledge, the more experience one obtains -the more one needs -there is only for-ward to move -but more where and how? Especially in a world (or at least a country) that underestimates one's desire for something beyond cars, homes, credit cards, money. It doesn't provide for those who want something lasting, something deep -a cause and reason. When you want something more this world creates discouragement because it just doesn't provide the means. So for people like us, we must create our own means, and this cause frustration, because if we knew what the means was we wouldn't be restless! Even more difficult is keeping the desire (for more) alive when following the norm would be so easy (but just because it's the norm doesn't mean it is right). One needs to keep strength and faith and meet more people similar to self.

I want you to keep this letter so anytime you feel that you're alone in the world, you can pick up and realize that you're not.

...Once I started talking to you, I realized that you were a lot like me and that I was a lot like you. Both of us considered to be different weird -according to the normal standard of society. However, being strangely and philosophically rational on a different level, we are both aware of the stagnant and rigid state of mind of the world. Neither of us is afraid to break out of the mold to be ourselves. I choose to call it "uniquely closer to perfection".

You probably never come to Germany again. The world is too big, too open for individual exploration and interpretation, too full of exciting and thought provoking experiences to stay in one place. The only place that I really want to stay is in your heart and mind. That's where you will be for me. If we should never meet on this planet again in the physical sense, and you need to find me, just take a trip to the world of dreams, to the deepest subterranean levels of your vast consciousness and call me. I will be there.

You came along at a crazy time in my life. I feel more comfort-able in knowing that you understand this without knowing all the details of my life. Life's nonsensical details are merely the reflection of the deeper, innermost battles we go through in our souls. You have been there on the sidelines, encouraging me with your own thoughts. Sometimes, you've been there right on the battle ground with me, helping me to find new strategies necessary to conquer the invisible opponents of the mind. I'm glad that there's someone else in this crazy world that understands my mind. Thank you. I never had a friend like you. One with whom I could just talk to, sinking from the surface of life's troubles to the deeper, darker, unknown depths of each other's minds. I don't talk to anyone else like how I talk to you. They are too scared of the unknown, too frightened of their own mind to become one with it. Their daily chores and idol desires are a refuge against the raging seas of thoughts deep within.

They become intimidated by my desire to investigate those crevices of their mind that they are unwilling to explore themselves. They become terrified when they see the deepness of my mind because I have chosen to express it through conversation. You are not scared to challenge those sometimes-turbulent waters within yourself and within me.

You have told me many times that you appreciate and admirer my intelligence. I know that you are able to do this because you, yourself, understand that this is the true state of living; the pursuit of knowledge and greater wisdom. This understanding is what motivates and guides you in your journey to find answers to those sometimes unasked and seemingly unanswerable questions in life. I appreciate your company because on our journeys I have learned more about myself and about those individualized characteristics that form my whole person. You are in control of your own journey. Where you want to go, you will go. What you seek to find, you will find. What you want to know, you will know. Do not be confused. The obstacles that will be placed in your path are necessary, yet can be overcome -if and only if you remember to too never relinquish the control that you have over you. Don't be afraid of emotion. As you have shown me, you have the courage to explore your own thoughts and my thoughts. You, therefore, have the tools to explore that other universe of untamed emotional seas.

If you ever need a voice of insane comfort if or when you become frustrated and seeming unfruitful in your search, come and fine me. You know where. I hope I have been as much inspiration to live and to think and to search beyond life's weak boundaries of logic and rationality, as you have been to me. It is on this level where our minds had frequently met, often enlightened each other, frequently led each other out of the dark unknown to greater and illuminated paths of wisdom. Like a friend -for that's what we are and what I hope we will always be.

Poetry

IT

The sun, moon and stars bare witness to it

How strong is it?

Nor was this constructed for me to become addicted to it

Of course she reflects it

Mystical is it

I refuse to run away with it

In her silent moments she nurtures it

The most important thing in her life is it

Too powerful for many to balance it

If they are not ready, I advise them not to touch it

Many ego-tripped with it

Sojourner risked her life for it

Martin died for it

Jesus revolutionized our hearts and minds with it

There isn't enough ink in the world to express it

Maybe she and I can embody and soul it

However, in my dreams I shall forever respect it

The world sings carols when celebrating it

Charity was born twin to it

I guess now I should identify it

Love is it

This Mind of Mine

one season must die before the other is born

nothing is concrete but the slabs in a foundation

until earth tremors awaken

wisdom nurtures me throughout the storm and knowledge

provides the shelter

fatigue is mystical

she is faceless and to my surprise

I submit to her wishes on a daily basis

she calls me when I don't have time

she wants to love me in the most inconvenient places

she kisses my soul and I slowly fall into a deep sleep

my words are recycled into the cycles of nature

just as a tree has withstood the death of many seasons understands its

place in nature

my energy is concentrated, transformed and supervised by a

critical perspective

could life be a journey guided into a quest, made to be truth,

tortured by reality, censored by perception, perfected by the thinker?

I escaped from my mother's womb unharmed

subject to the laws of man

the garden of life is where gentle feet walk

the mind is where intellect is stalked

The Powerful Union (English Version)

Fashioned by the laws of the cosmos, balanced with the thoughts of a god, planting knowledge seeds in my lover's womb, in order to bring forth truth, high flying with the birds from the jungles of wisdom

My lover is made whole when I crown her woman of the universe, giver of the ultimate pleasure. Respecting myself for I am the keeper of her peace, as she stands as the supreme keeper of her man. No mysteries will infiltrate our confidence in the union of our souls. The scent from her body erupts into the atmosphere giving pleasure and moisture to my nostrils. I stand on mountaintops looking down on from which I came, af-ter being buried in a womb, born from a tomb. My lover and I soar hand in hand through oceanic dreams filled with mystical wishes. We hold liba-tions for the ancestors buried in the land of hoary. Our castle will be built from alpha stones and our kingdom will be built from omega bricks. The light of wicked men will shine upon our crowns, but our queendom will be impenetrable. Our orchards will mirror those of heaven. I have progressed from an ovum to a king, so I stand as a confident warrior prepared to conquer your heart. We shall transplant our love from the body of the finite into the body of the infinite, in order to advance beyond earthly limitations. A revolution will take place in my lover's mind causing a rotation back to the essence of self-consciousness. Understanding we shall come and go, we must live this earth journey to the fullest so when we are called back to the realm of eternal peace, the gods will have a celebration on our behalf.

Millennium Queen of Heaven

reaching out over the horizon

Tongue kissing female rainbow spirits

Millennium wishes falling from dreamy skies

Nobody knows so I lie on my back screaming silently

for my shadow mistress

She walks in and reaches out for me

Soft touches showering my physical with electric raindrops

My boots are heavy

My thoughts are infamous Clydesdale stampeding through western chronicle

My emotions are fallen like snow

My feelings accumulate around my feet

freezing the liquid justice in my world

Untamed fears soaring above my head like thunder clouds gliding in and out of cyberspace realities

Beyond midnight hills where fantasies are activated

Nobody seems to believe internal personalities are dogmatic when fishing for private company

While demons masquerade into our private thoughts claiming to be law Watch your soul and guide your emotions

When your spirit reaches out over the horizon in search of millennium love

Excerpt from the poem: 189 Travels with Xes

...the man begins to slip into the darkness of his mind

his eyes become useless so he puts them to sleep

his intuition becomes his guide leading him to the flood plains lying beneath the belly of a black earth

Within that soft warm place, the warrior is awakened and realizes that the feminine waters over flowing from her

womanish flood plains is the signal needed

before entering the sensuality of Erotica

the warrior has slipped into the playground of the gods

the place where the ancestors cultivate fruit

fruit filled with cosmic sensations exploited by the hearts of men and woman on timeless travels.

Excerpt from the poem: Love Fantasy

... her love is exotic because it dances effortlessly and nude

until my hormones give a standing ovation

Men can hunt me down and capture my wealth

However

Never will they separate me from my true treasure

My infinite pleasure

She is my wisdom tree

Deep rooted in my love fantasy

Pink Sunshine Emotions

P.S.E.

It is a love war, reverse it, rewind it, research it, deny it

Blind hearts always find it

Dripping with hope, addictive wonderful dope

Which flavor you crave?

Do not eat it too fast

You may evoke rage

It shall carry you into forward motion

Constantly moving you into reversing it

Rewinding it, researching it, denying it

Sincere hearts are sometimes tortured by it

Researching it

I find it in many forms

Blowing as storms, maybe calm, silent, just the norm

Whatever information fits your current motivation

Pink sunshine emotions best define love situations

My Angel the Ageless Jewel

Celebrate with me as her body fragrance travels through my nostrils until it becomes a living spirit of pleasure

Searching through the blackness of antiquity- marvelously in harmony with the universe

She stands as pieces of earth mixed with wonderful juices of love, seasoned with drops of ethnic sovereignty

The words she speak are Nubian entities

Encouraging Earth dwellers to wind down to the music of windstorms, so behold with attention for she loves deep with metaphysical laws of justice, so now I wander in the waters of the abyss

Upon the boat of ebony pleasure, aloof from the world

Observe again as she blows beautiful midnight colors into my mind, causing me to blindly search through perfume enriched rhythms for temples of peace, her image fluctuates in the raven river of infinity

She stands in the mist of my mind on fertile soil

Watch as admirable beauty is harvested in thy mind

Like crops from the field, wonderful agriculture with melanin features cultivated by the hands of the goddess

My angel I propose a man to be energy molded into flesh

Walking the earth electrifying the atmosphere in some form or fashion, tamed only by the light reflecting from the jewel of ageless wisdom

Excerpt from the poem: What is the profit of a mind that gains the world and forgets about the soul?

... silver and gold bureaucracies unfold, elaborating upon a certain mind state. Material desires, along with mystical, egotistical power fixations fuel my attention, guiding my desire for the ultimate treasure hunt.

Excerpt from the poem: The Millennium Season of Autumn

Everything comes into check upon my stressful crown; cashing in reality bonds for my soul's investment in a cultural renaissance.

My government is aggressive and guided by searchers of wealth

my soul is the jewel

my flesh is the chest

A nation lives through the mind and is energized by the soul, guided by the spirit. So my logic performs an exodus into the future, constructing-preparing an Abyssinian kingdom for my arrival.

N.F.B.T.I.

Navigating far beyond the immediate

Puncturing holes in society with razor sharp beliefs backed by natural facts. For years oppressed people cried freedom, so now they bleed insurrection. Spirits of resistance haunt the guilty perpetrators in their anti-freedom assemblies. Wandering minds from D.istant C.orners search deep into the asylum of the wicked finding new and improved ways to run this society. No one dares to be brave enough to unleash the swiftness of the tongue on the obesity and slothfulness of ignorance. We are all responsible for our actions and lack of actions. My expressions are calm and ready to move into the field of combat. My subconscious dances to the rhythm of insight and bonds with the genes of the universe. I believe cause and effect will run wild and untamed forever begging those who instituted the cause to ready themselves for the effects. Navigating far beyond the immediate bring-ing distance between myself and stagnate mind states.

Earth Soldier

Surrender your mind and listen closely when silent tongues prepare to speak upon the truth

Watch as their words attempt to decipher meanings

Sending affirmations quietly gliding across the immeasurable corridors of intelligence within the psyche

Speaking to a select few

Evoking the spirits of freedom to battle in the war for Earth

Dandelions of power mixed in with flowers of ecstasy are found growing in the courtyards of hoary

Behold the soldiers kneeling at the feet of the empress of antiquity dripping with the life fluid of condemned souls

These soldiers are asking to be cleansed

with the kiss of peace before entering the temples of melanin

While there, soldiers study the true science of harmony within the

energy levels of nature and listens to the faint heartbeat of Earth

Until the war continues

Truth hovers the skies of heaven revealing

a non-stop confrontation lies with the rising of the sun and sets with casualties of the soul

Surrender your mind and listen closely when silent tongues

prepare to speak upon the truth

Evoking the spirits of freedom to battle in the war for Earth

777 sages ago

when we met upstairs

before we ascended to the heavens

I found her in the midnight hours

traveling from derelict to priest

night sounds and sweet swells elevating our sensual appetite for one another

Al-Sirat is where her essence dwells

together we search for that hidden place

her ecstasy is natural – never governed by mint

heaven sent from the Earth like I came

we both once again resurrected by Gaia

when we met upstairs

before we ascended to the heavens

she shares with me the secrets of hoary

as I take her through my internal dream kingdom

she first allows me to touch her physical

marveling after her beautiful body

evoking the interest of all 7 senses

then my queen disappears into me- teaching me how to feel my lord she satisfies me through the element of fire

when we met upstairs

before ascending to the heavens

Look hard enough and...

Enter the realms of mental stamina and discover new unauthorized territories of mind control. Unattended minds wilt like lifeless trees because they lack the fortified culture needed to nurture their roots and neutralize negativity. The mind is the supreme explorer shedding light on the path of those individuals with injured realities looking to be healed by ultimate truth. Citizens are hypnotized by madness and breast-fed violence so no one is surprised when supervised massacres become a reality. Society has fallen short of truth and grown too tall for justice. Behold when intelligent tongues speak forcing wickedness back into its tomb of destruction. Ignorance skinny dips in the rivers of society feeling no shame for his vulgar actions because barbarians justify his motives and awards him with the trophy of ethnocide. The masses are easily relaxed by the slumberous words of elected hypocrites and the story goes on unless...

Insert from the poem:
Afronectar Verse 7: 9-13

"...their firstborn are cosmic messiahs, heavenly seeds preparing to bloom in the millennium of the sun cycle. Wise men gather there around tribal fires telling the story of a strange woman named Armageddon, who married a prince of the Equinox Mysteries. Of-course these are the secret doctrines the Cushite Queens are warring to protect. So I ask again, what information you are seeking when your thoughts journey beyond obscure freedom dreams, refusing to be tamed..."

My queen needs to know

I've built a bride for you and I
in order that we may send pieces of love to one another across life's troubled waters
intricately woven healing herbs shall be used
as blankets for warming our cold souls
together we can manufacture pieces of power in our
factories of liberation
growing into a bond sealed by the blood of deceased kin
so now let us manifest truth through the winds of trouble until
our bond with the Creator provide the means for escape
never bothered by the petty definitions of love
invented by those ignorant dweller of chaos
we sit together and watch the gods perform miracles
in the cathedrals of equality
we will nurture our bodies with dynamic fruit growing
in the gardens of heaven
just forward your thoughts into my heart and I will operate
until I build your short-comings into a beautiful temples of love
I'm the blackest earth bound soul ordained by the power of the true
God of royal light
come and we will swim in oceans of laughter
after walking the shores of reality

true real, black pearls

mistakes will appear

we must oppose the general of non-forgiveness plan

to invade our love bond

remember the ancestors guide our every move

so let us stay in touch with our ethnic essence of divine revelation
which states

"God is the life force"

My king needs to know

Naturally the wind will blow
Naturally the sun will shine
So naturally
I willingly enlist my deepest feelings of desire
in the war for your kingdom
just crown me the queen of your heart
my lips are like two dark thunder clouds parting after a violent storm
bringing peace and tranquility
I will send my warriors to liberate you from the shackles of
uncertainty my king if you ever get stranded
call upon me and my words will rescue you
come into me and love my body
study my mind and I will quiz you on the grounds of forever
I am your spiritual chest
so search in me for your treasures
when you feel cold
I will call upon the sun to shine upon your brow
for God is good
look deep sweetheart and you will taste him in my smile

I am the feminine star that shines on your soft side

after the war

come lay with me in the garden and I will heal your wounds with pieces of paradise

sprinkle me over your life and I will make it feel so good my king

so good

Don Robinson • 53

www.ingramcontent.com/pod-product-compliance
Lightning Source LLC
Chambersburg PA
CBHW070102100426
42743CB00012B/2638